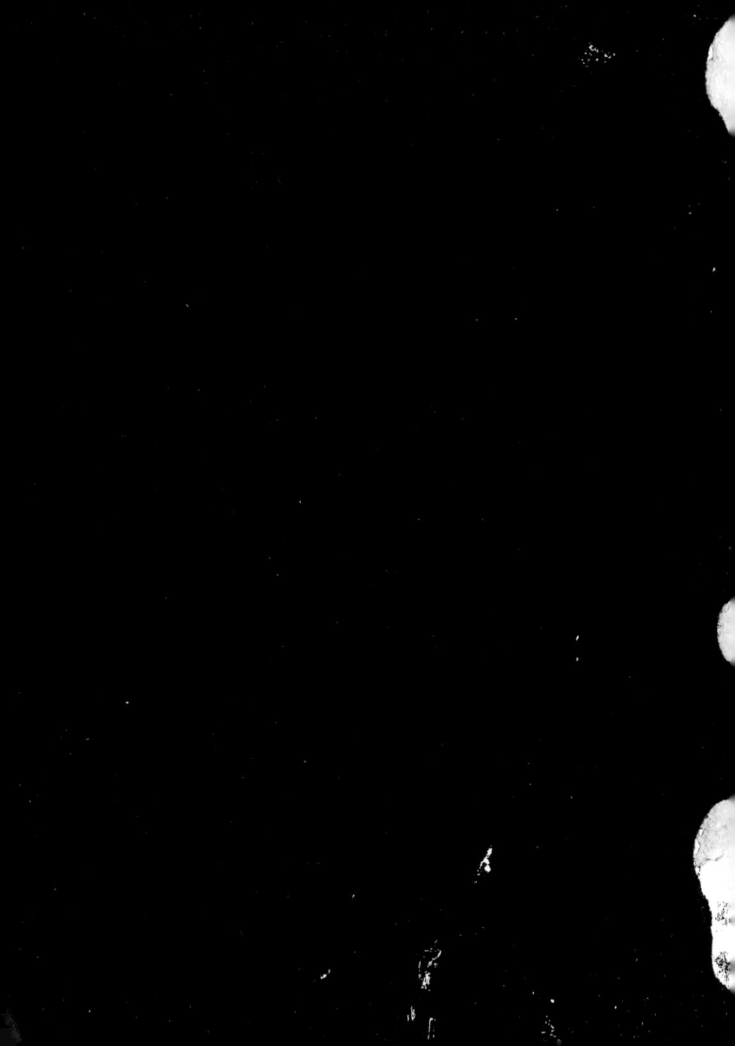

DANIEL BRUSH: THINKING ABOUT MONET

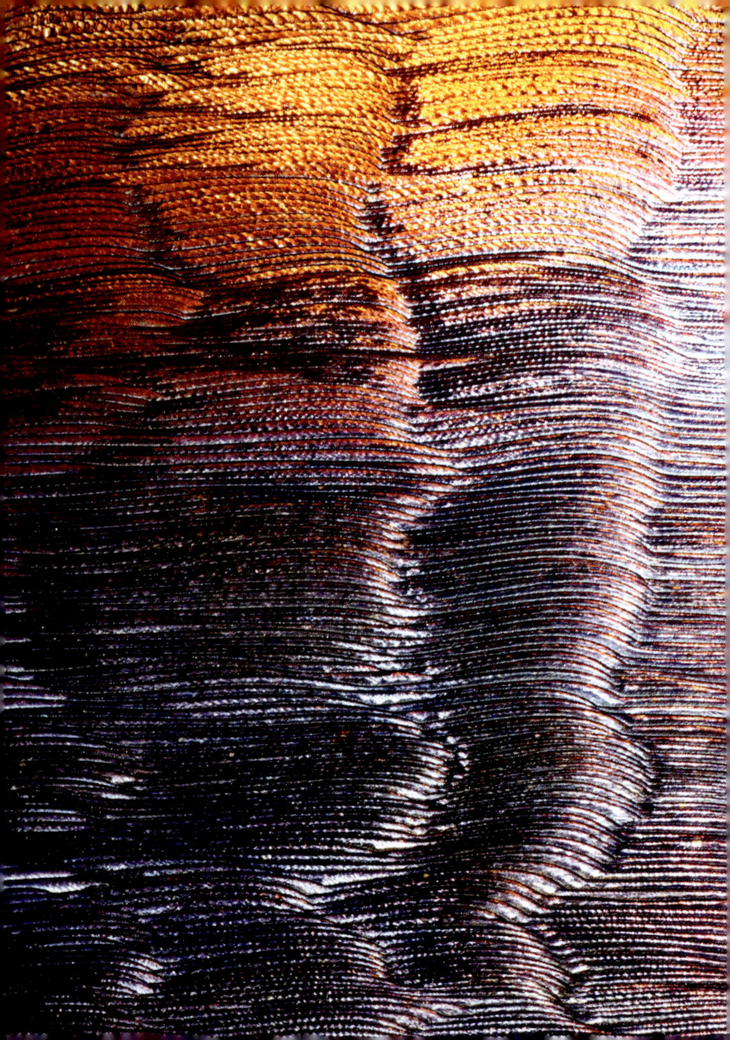

DANIEL BRUSH

THINKING ABOUT MONET

L'ÉCOLE, School of Jewelry Arts
MW Editions

PREFACE

Light was one of Daniel Brush's enduring preoccupations: the nature and science of light, its meanings, the responses it generates, the light within a gemstone, the light that his engraved aluminum brings to a woman's face, eyes, and skin. His fascination began in his high school and college physics lessons, when he saw how a light beam could be bent and refracted through the use of a diffraction grating, with its thousands of mechanically scored lines per inch.

Daniel was also intrigued by the French impressionists' use of color, particularly Monet's light-infused hues of muted pinks, cerulean blues, and cadmium yellows. He and Olivia, his wife, traveled to Europe many times in an effort to understand this very specific use of color. They spent several months living in Paris and visited Arles, Rouen, and the fields of Giverny, where

Monet painted his haystacks. Despite his fascination with Monet's technique, Daniel had an abiding distaste for the impressionist master's work. "Even with all those classical glazing techniques, the paintings did not have the majesty of the natural light bathing haystacks, the *meules de foin*, that we went to see in the fields," he remarked.

Back in Manhattan, a friend and art collector showed Daniel and Olivia an eight-by-ten-inch transparency of a Monet painting that he was considering acquiring. They held it up to the window to inspect the image, and in that moment, Daniel said, "I liked Monet's work when I saw it as a transparency with the light shining through."

In this series, Daniel paradoxically engraved the ephemerality of light in hard, dark steel. I hope that you are moved by this light as you take in these extraordinary works of art.

Nicolas Bos
President and CEO of Van Cleef & Arpels

THINKING ABOUT MONET: CAPTURING THE LIGHT

Everyone has a history.
With a nod to Proust, mine is a remembrance of things present.

Every summer Saturday and stretching into the fall, we were deposited at the Cleveland Museum of Art for drawing classes held in different galleries. We had black leatherette cases with Conté crayons, gum erasers, smooth and pebble paper pads, and Prang watercolor tins. His sister, older and into fashion, thought it was hilarious that we wore berets because artists were French. We hated all of it and stole away every time to the armor court to draw the knights, blunderbusses, and lances.

We had to leave the museum through the French impressionist galleries, and this is where I began to hate Monet. It was the pasty oil paint, the sweet colors, and the small sizes. We gorged ourselves at home on Necco wafers and candy dots, always thinking and laughing about Monet's colors.

Three years later, my mother took me to thirteen European countries in eleven days, checking off the must-sees. We stood in front of Monet's *Water Lilies* installed at l'Orangerie in Paris, she exclaiming and me still choking on the Necco wafer colors. However, on that trip I knew I would become an artist. My greatest possession for years was the Stanhope that I got as a souvenir from the Lido nightclub, which let me come of age many times and convinced me that Toulouse Lautrec's life was the one I wanted.

A collector asked me to join him at a prestigious gallery in New York City in 1986. He was considering the purchase of a Monet painting. I said no. Pushed, I sat next to him while he thought about living with the painting for six months. I hated the *meules de foin*! But when the dealer held up an eight-by-ten-inch transparency of the same painting, it stunned me. With the light coming through the image, the painting became extraordinary. Was this what Monet saw? Olivia and I traveled to Paris, Arles, Dieppe. We sat in front of the Rouen cathedral. We sat in the fields for hours, for days, looking at the shifting light on the haystacks.

I am obsessed with and seduced by the light that Monet saw. These steel sculptures are the beginning of my work.

Daniel Brush, 2020

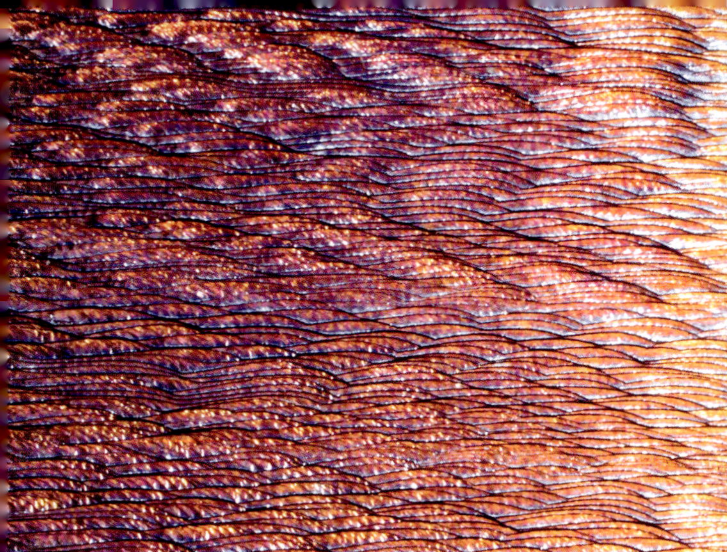

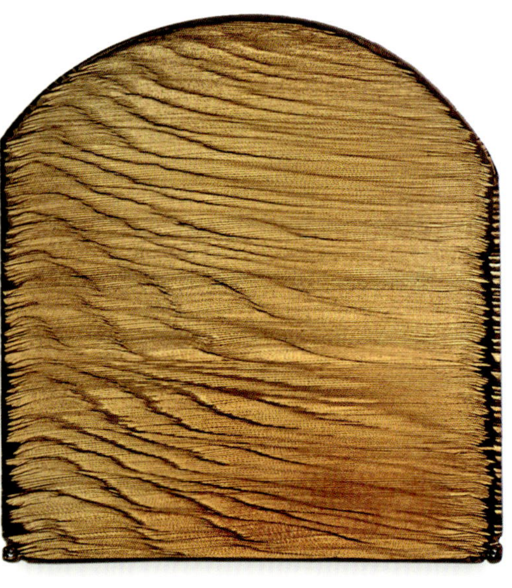

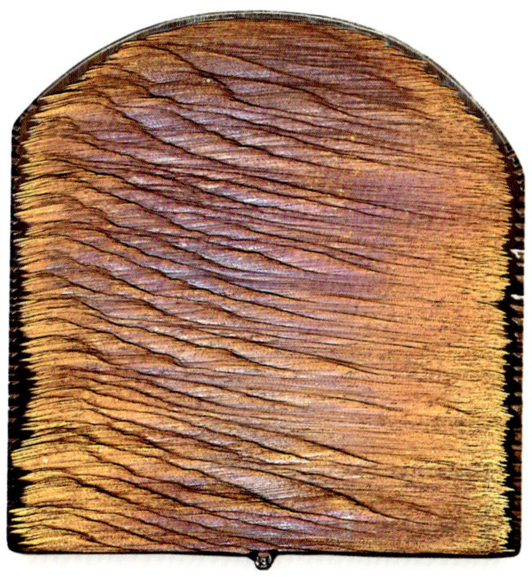

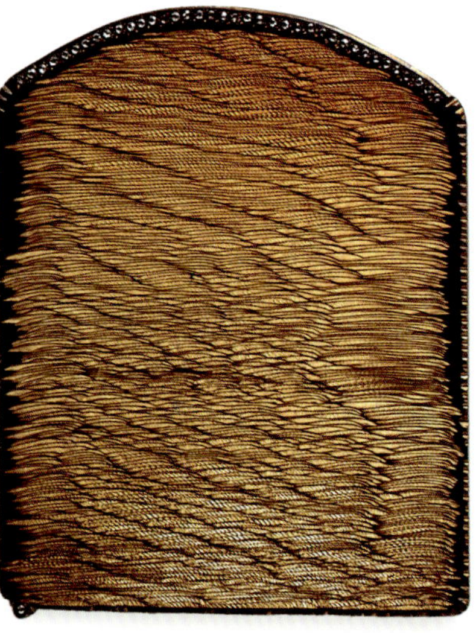

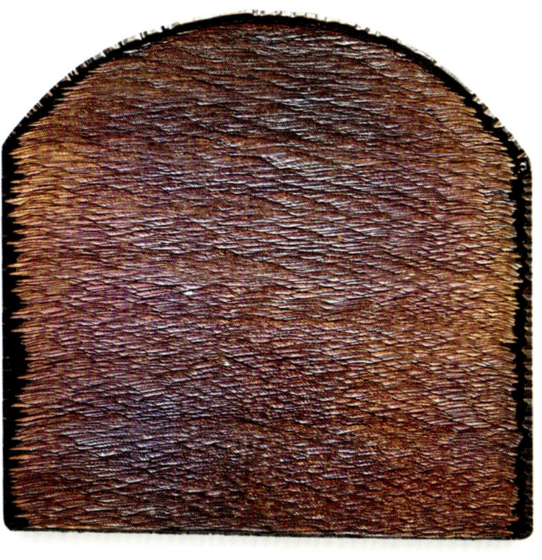

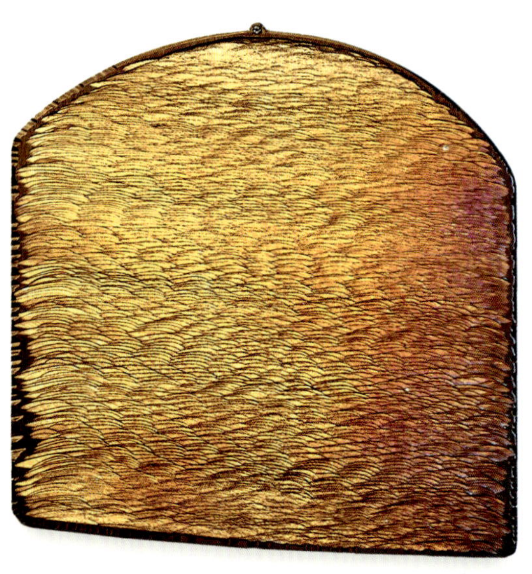

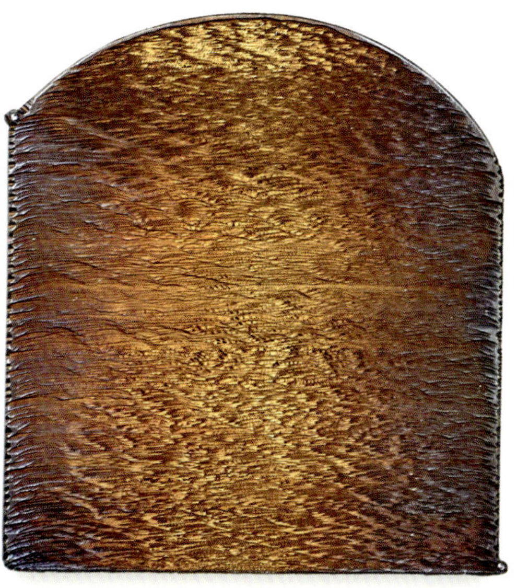

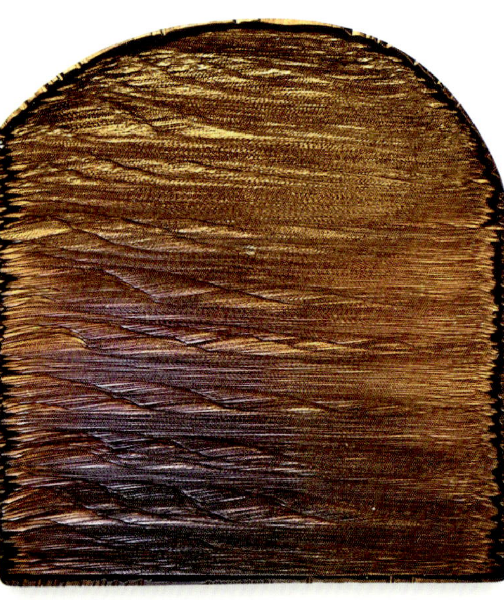

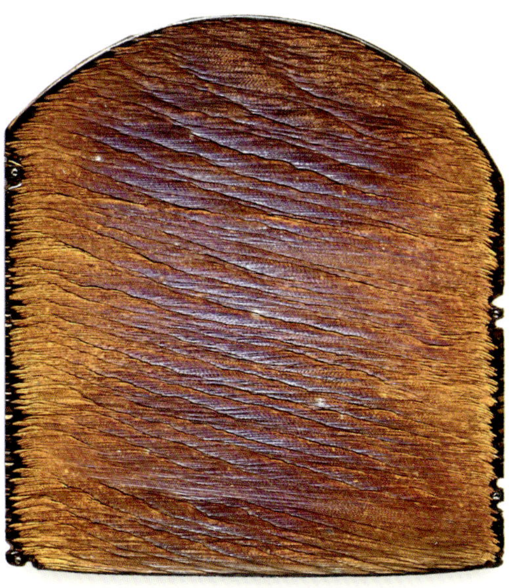

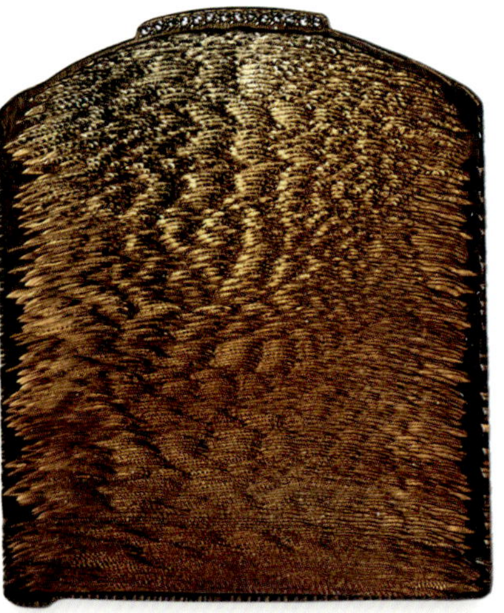

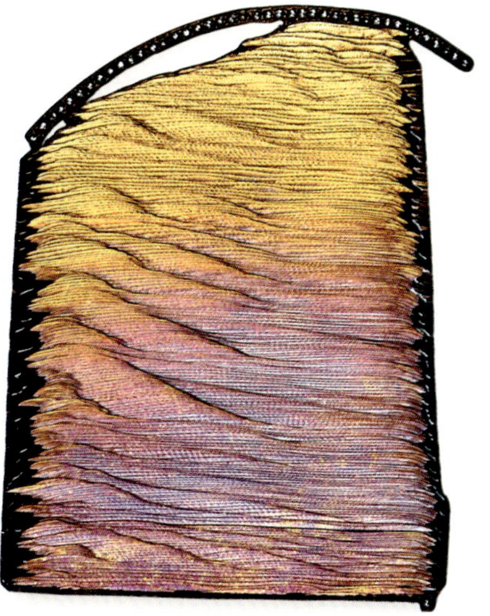

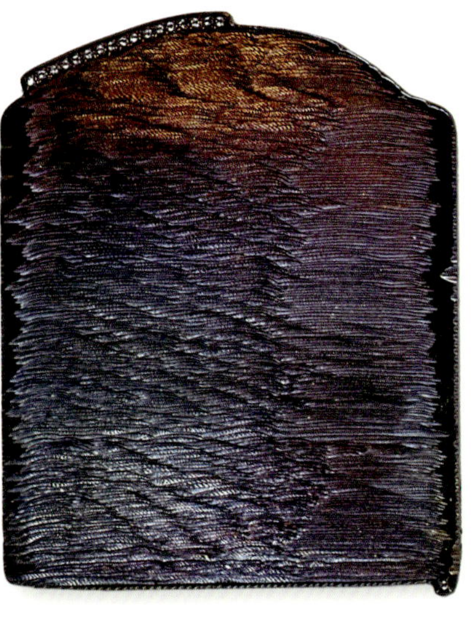

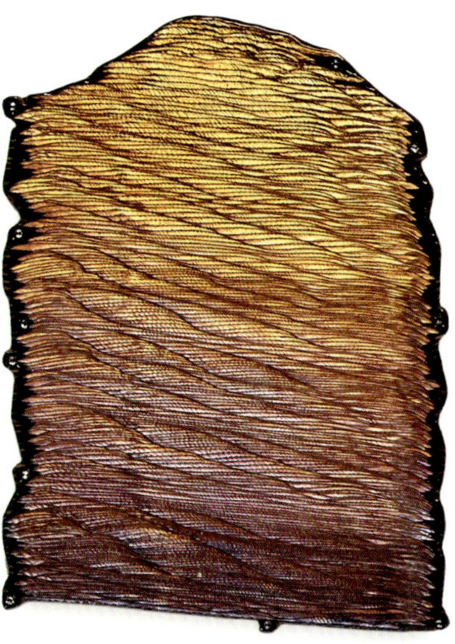

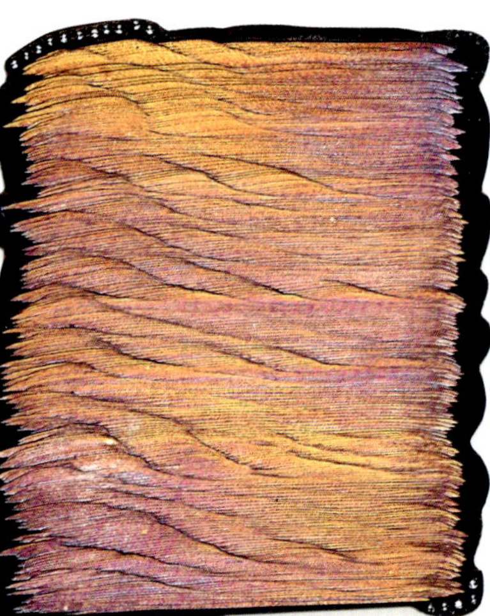

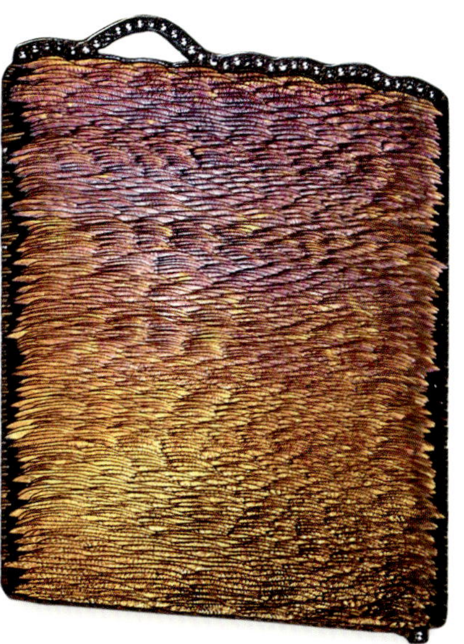

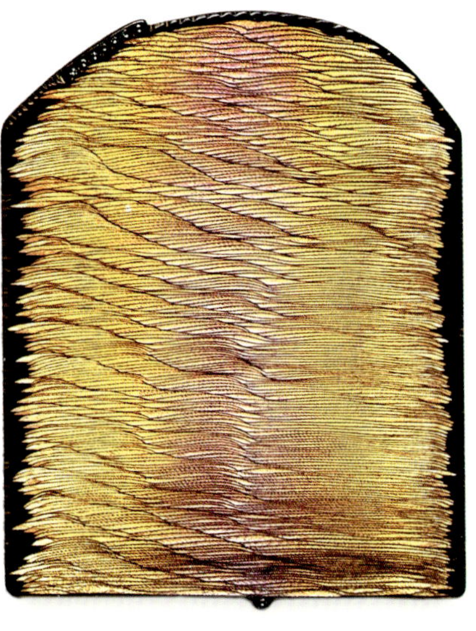

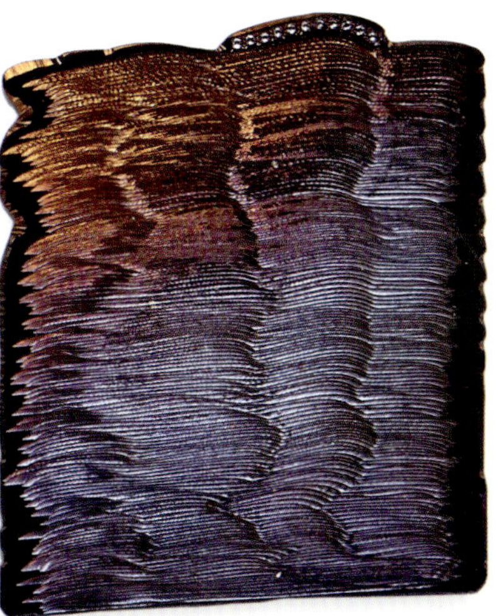

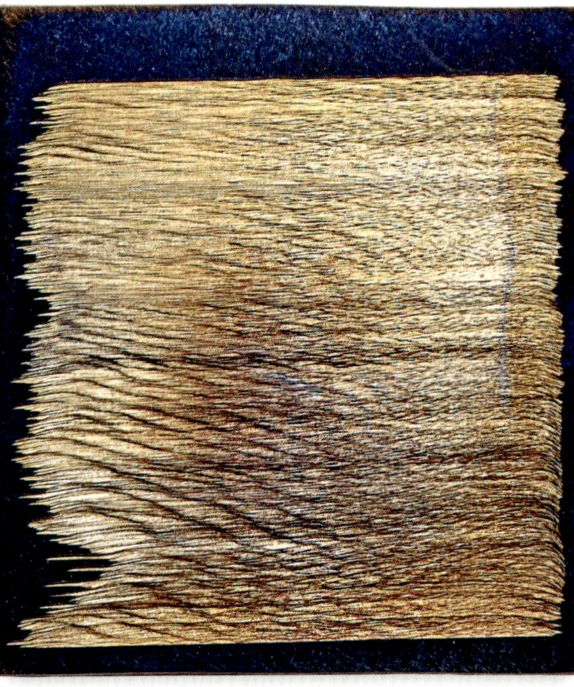

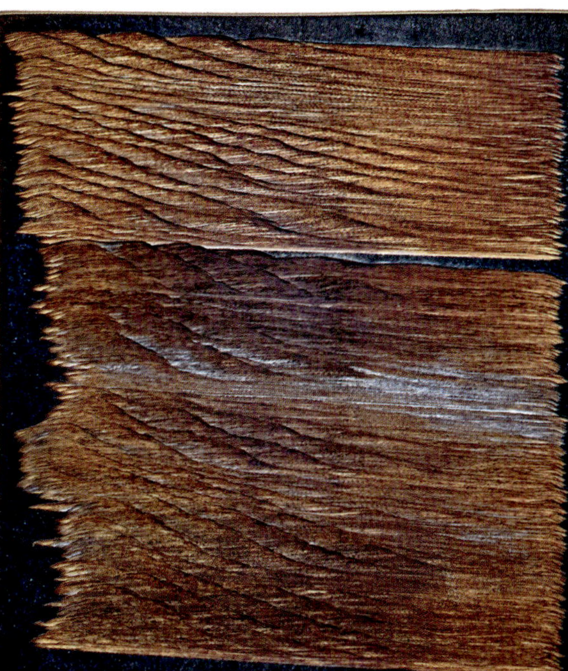

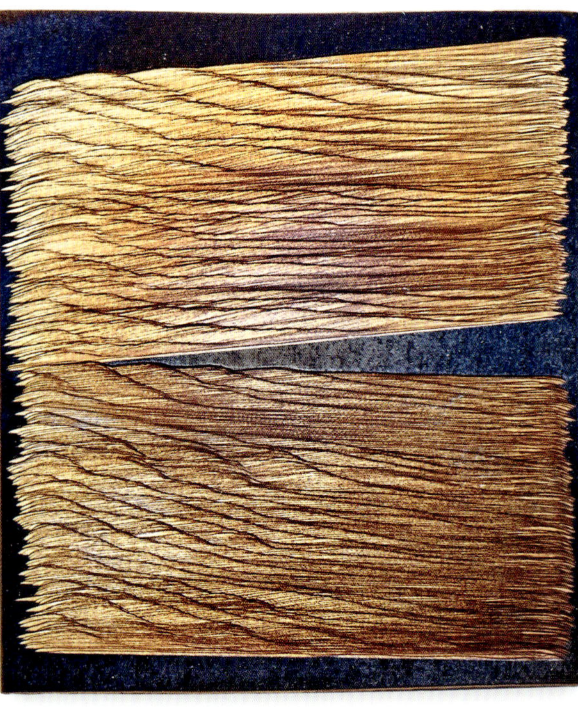

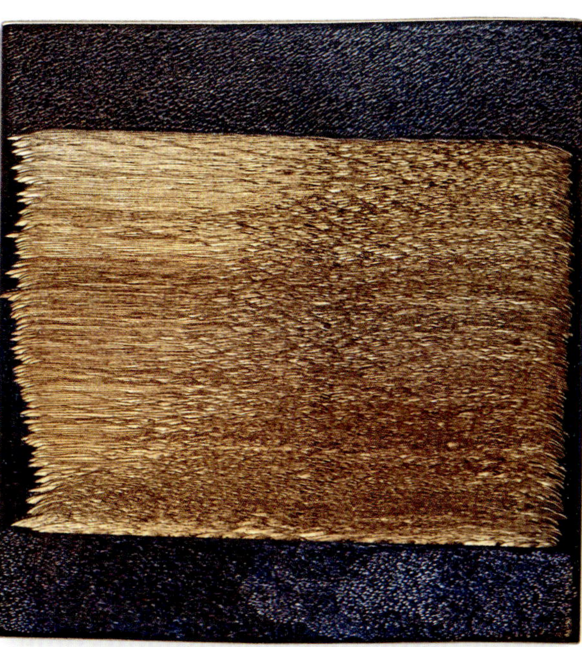

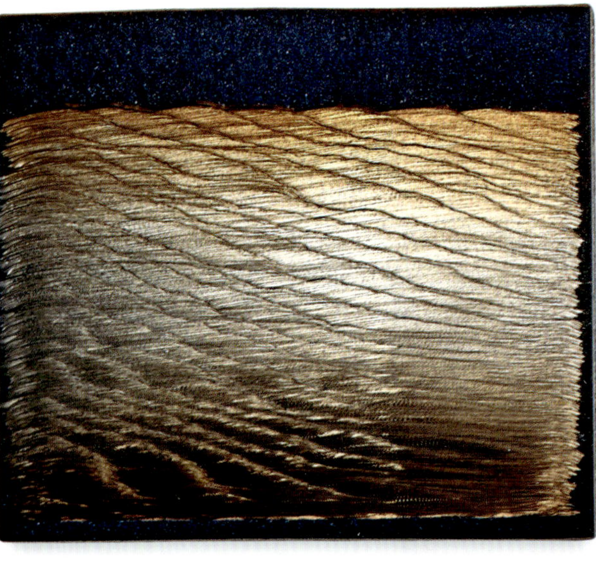

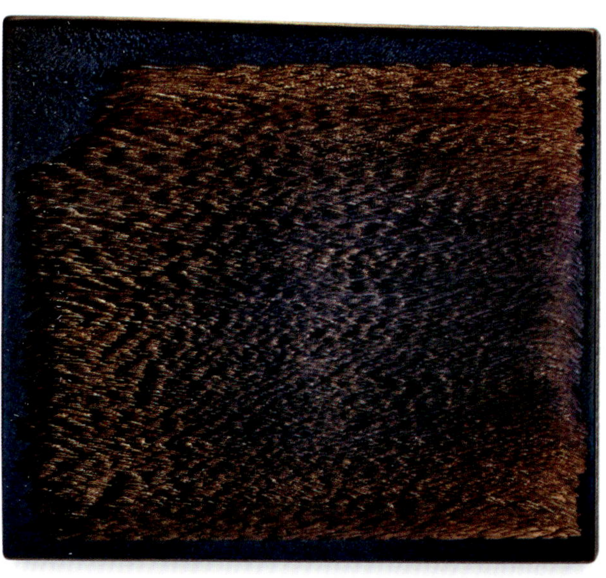

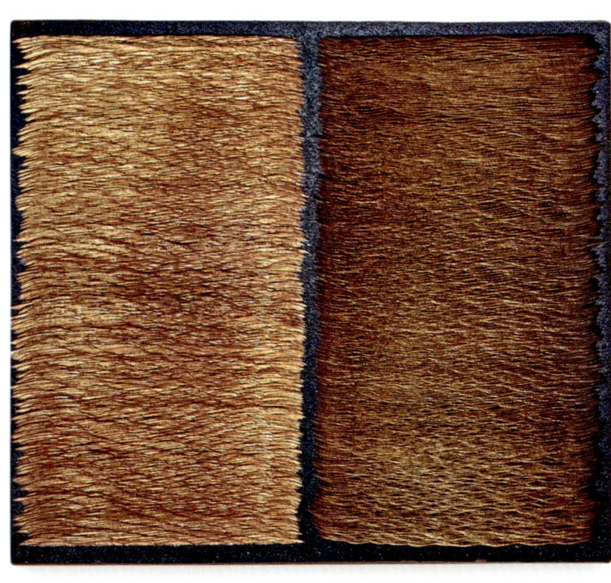

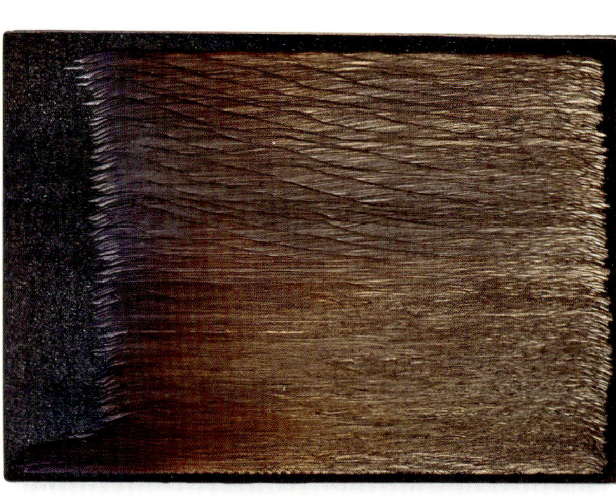

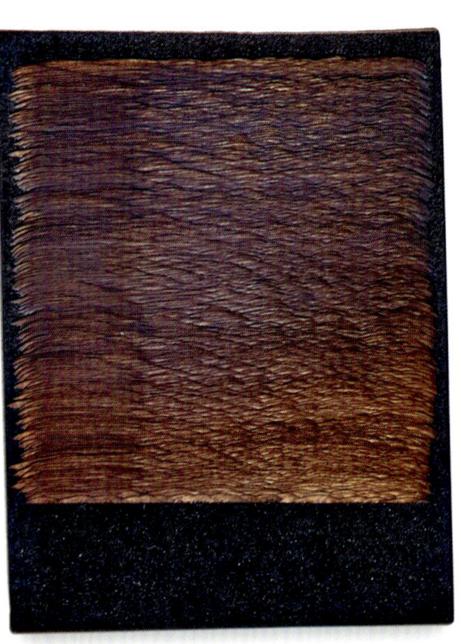

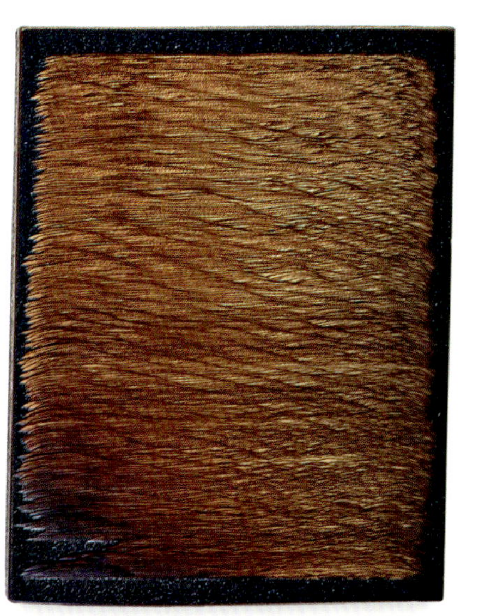

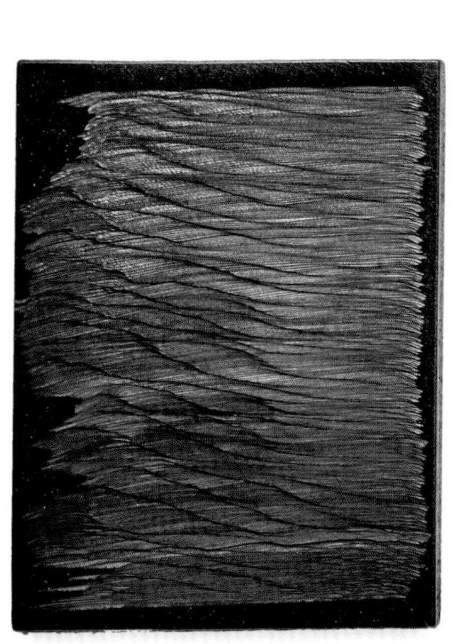

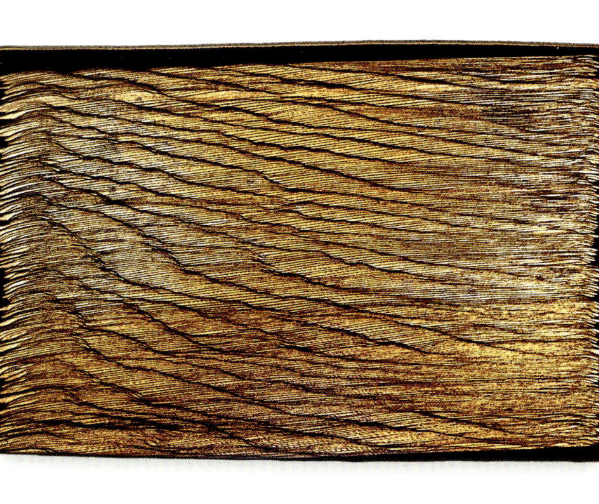

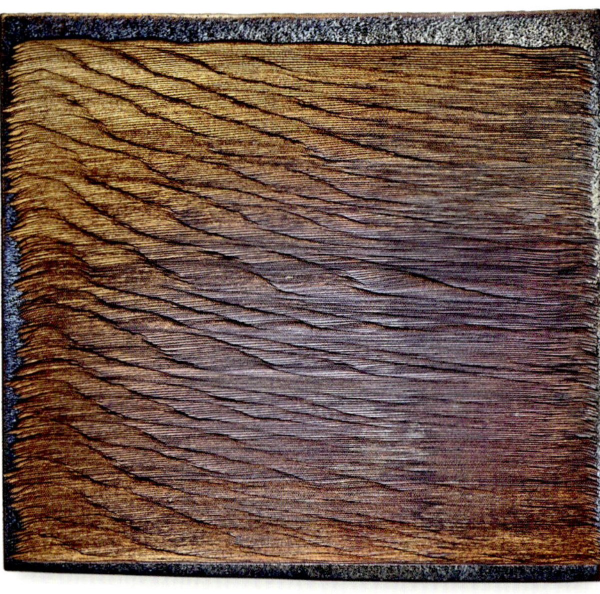

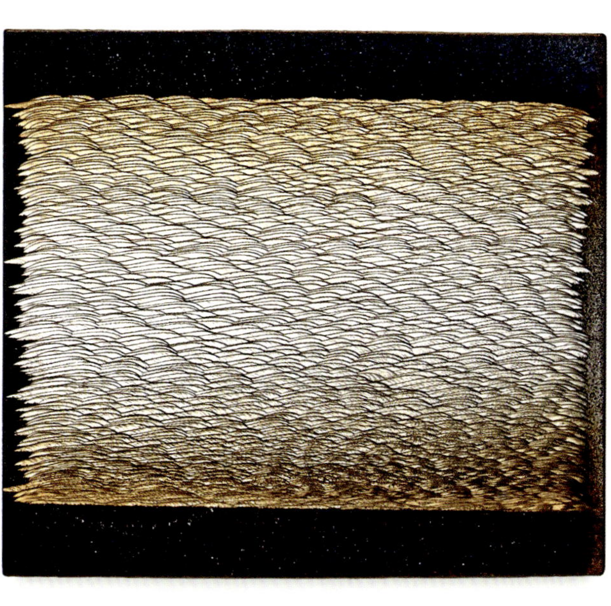

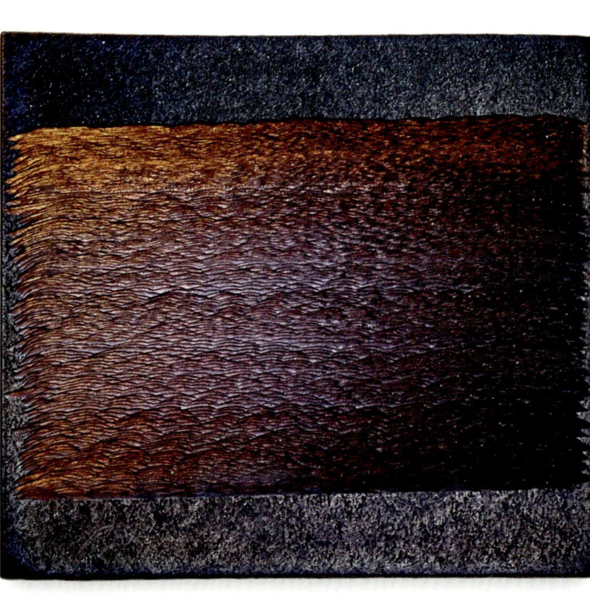

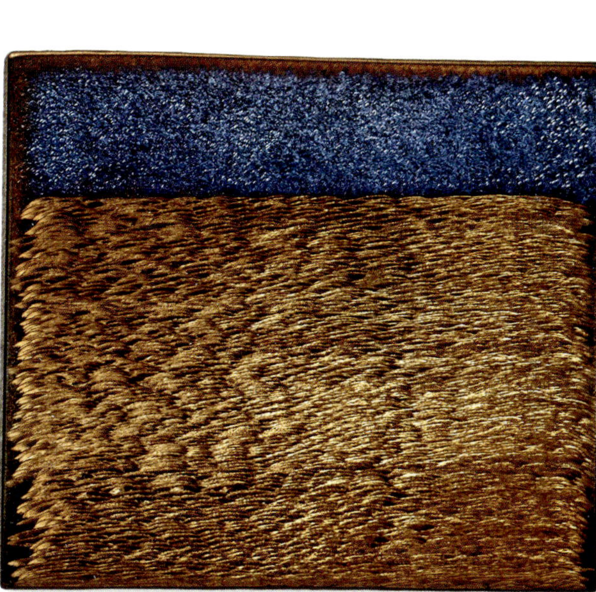

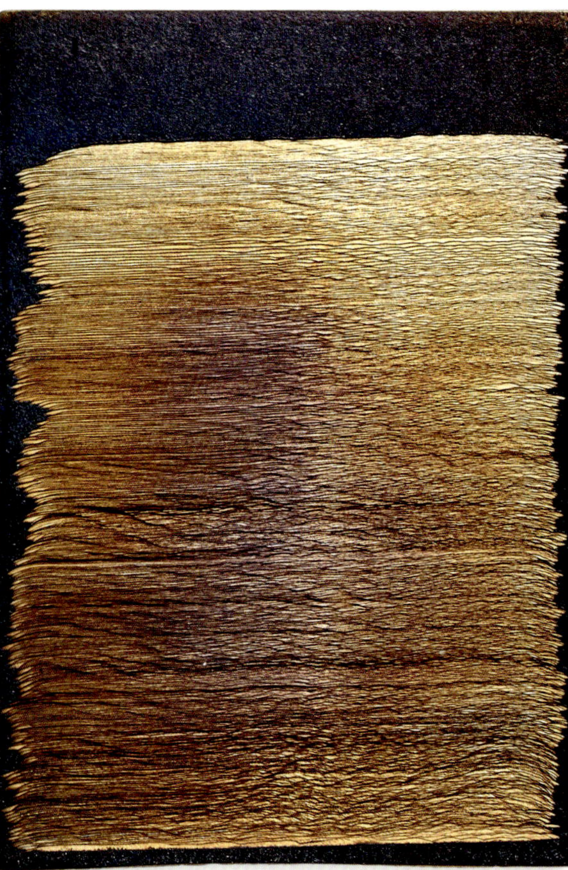

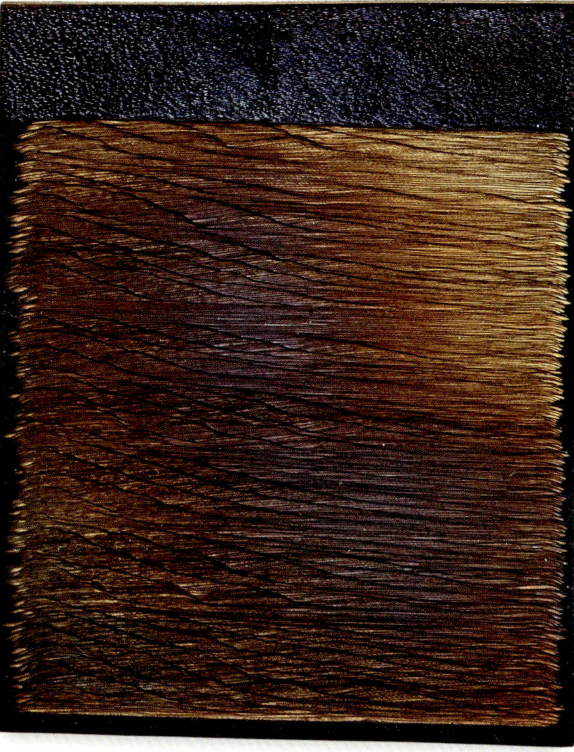

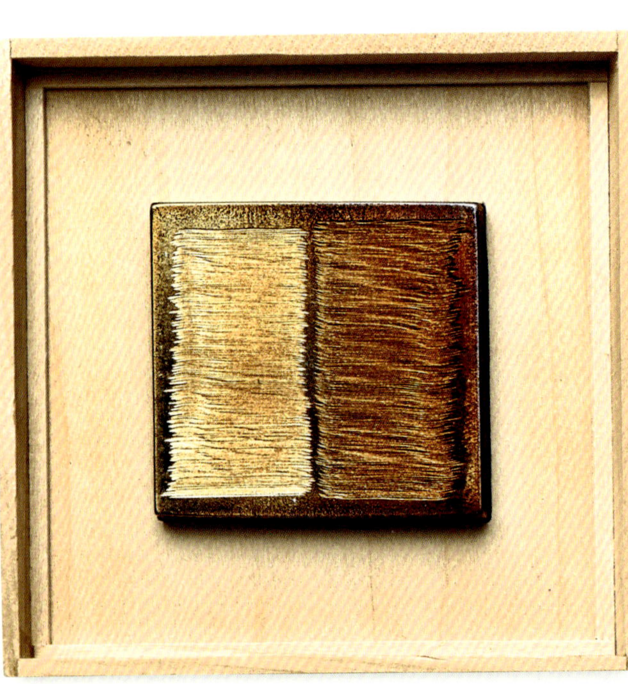

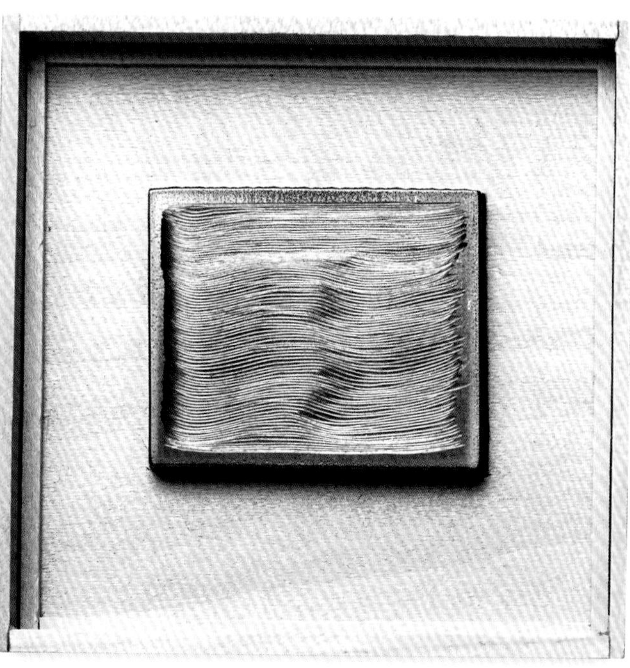

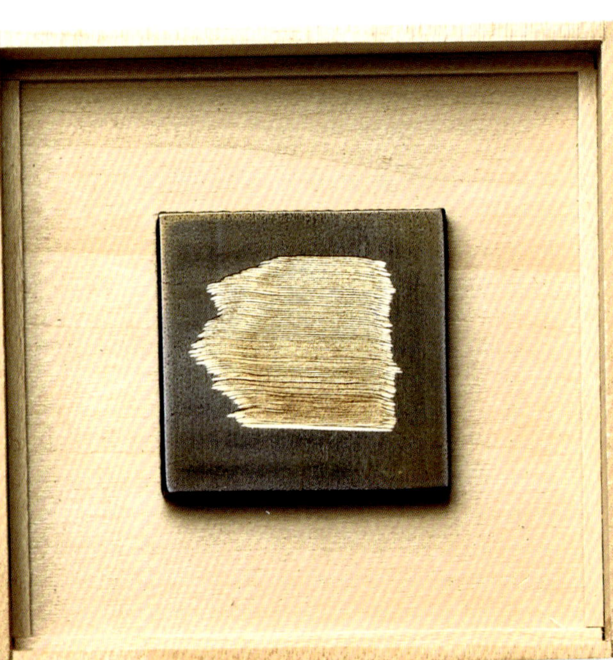

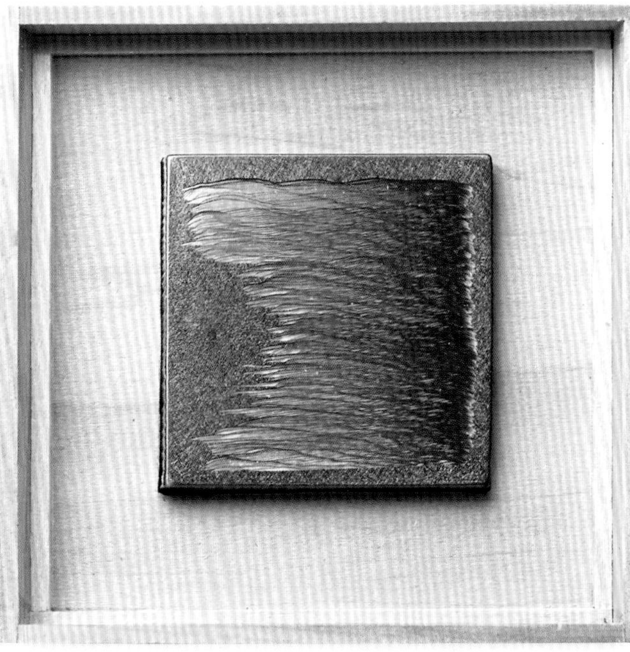

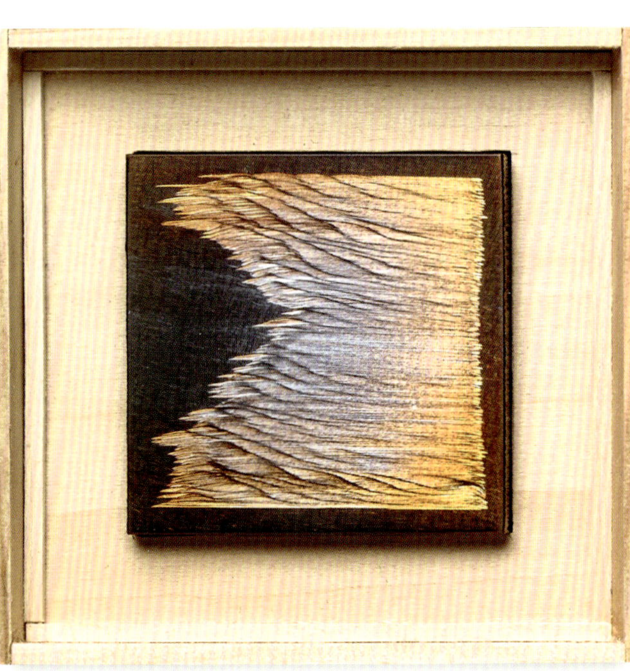

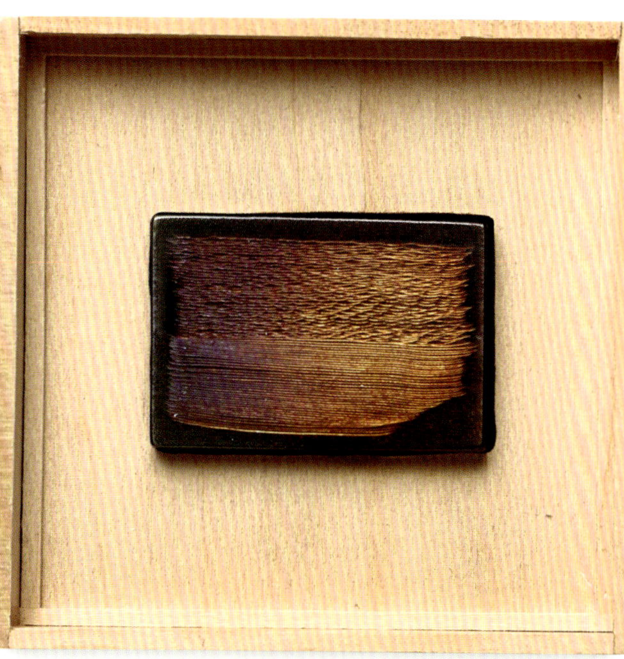

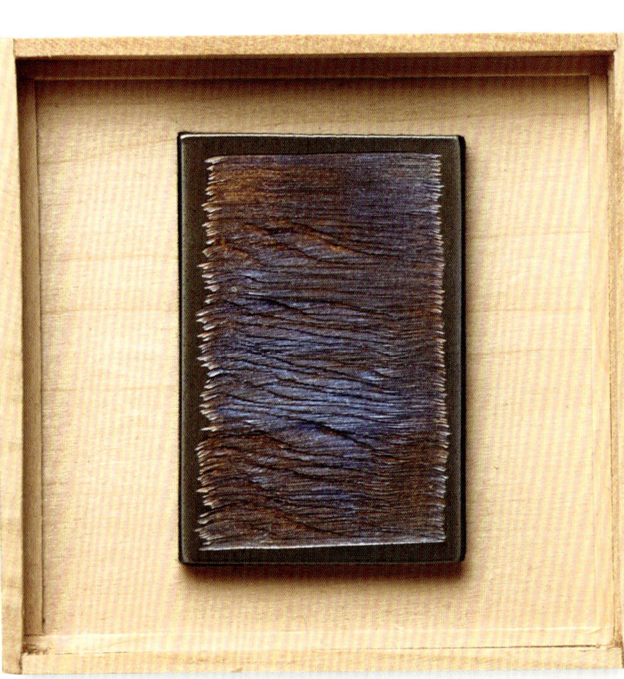

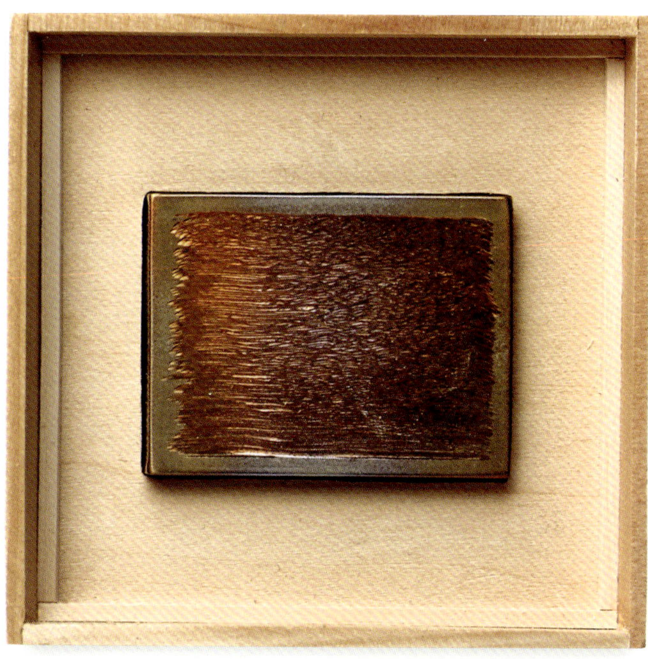

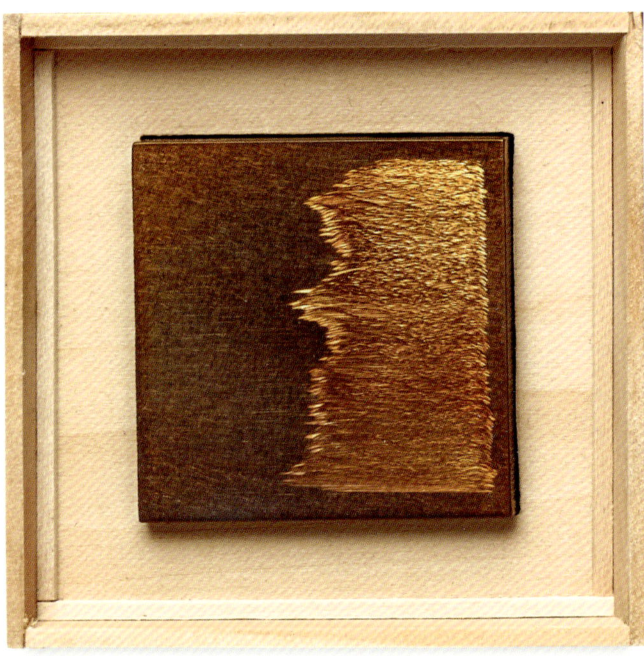

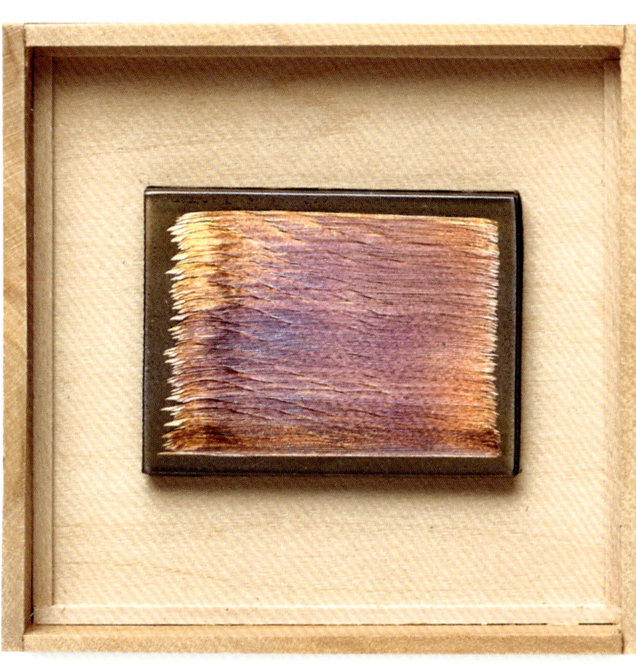

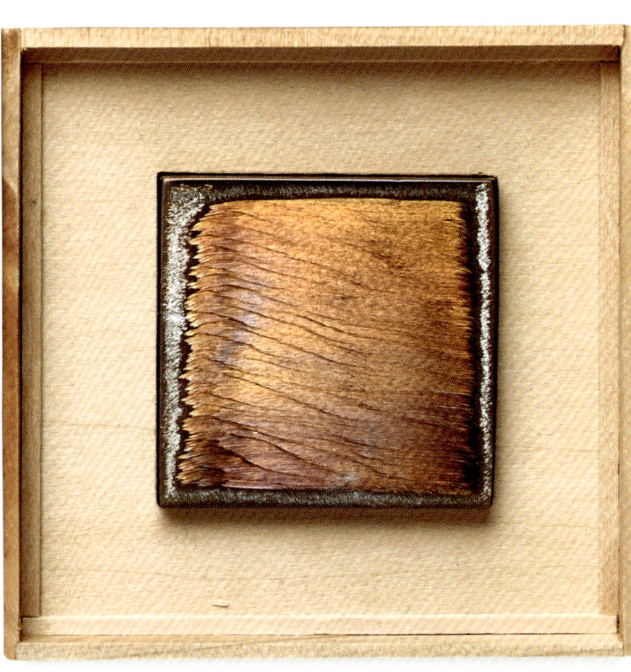

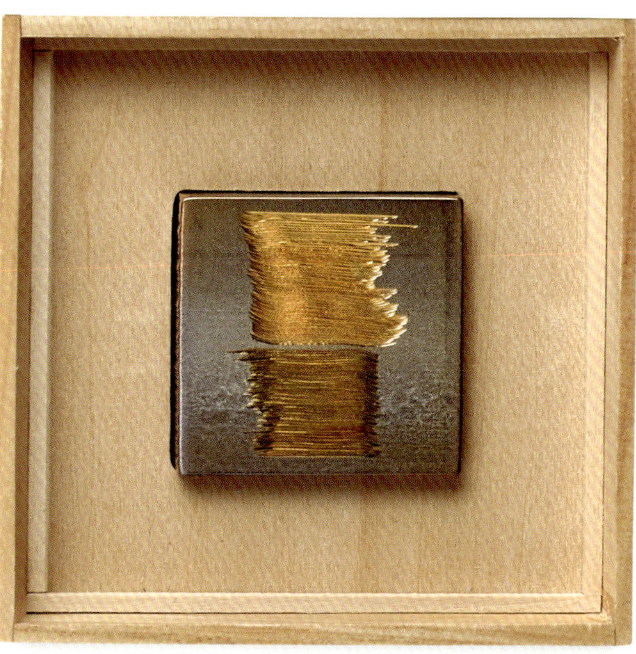

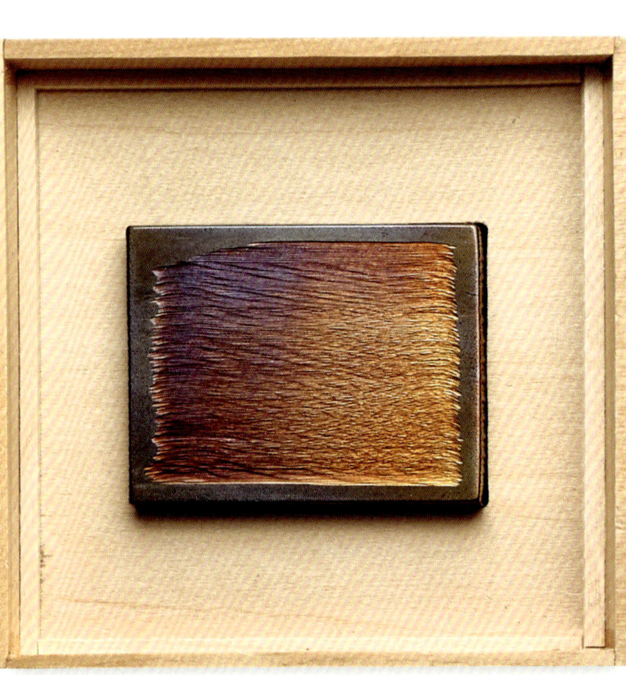

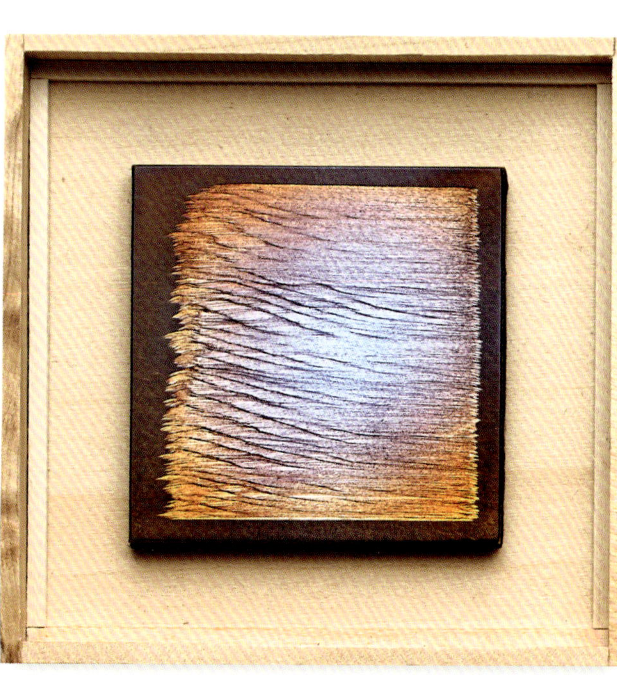

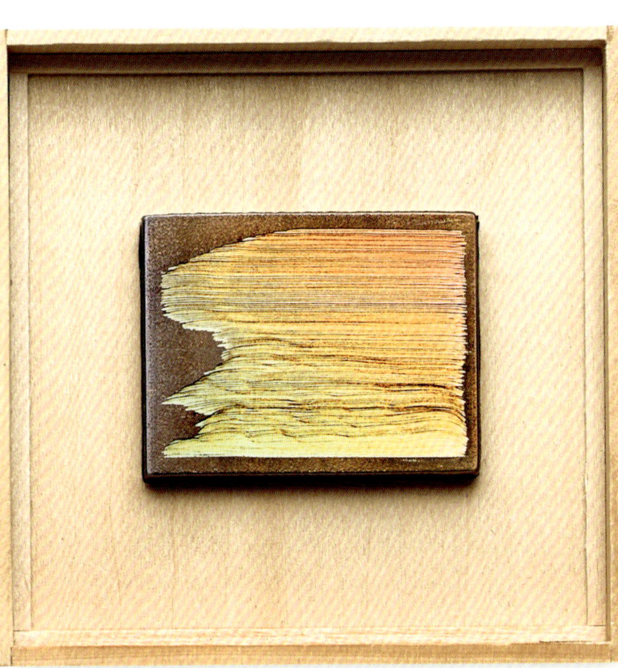

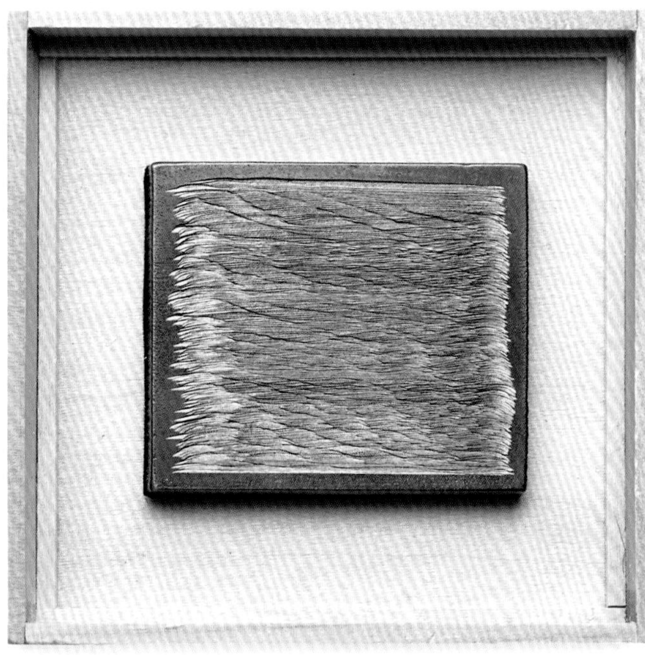

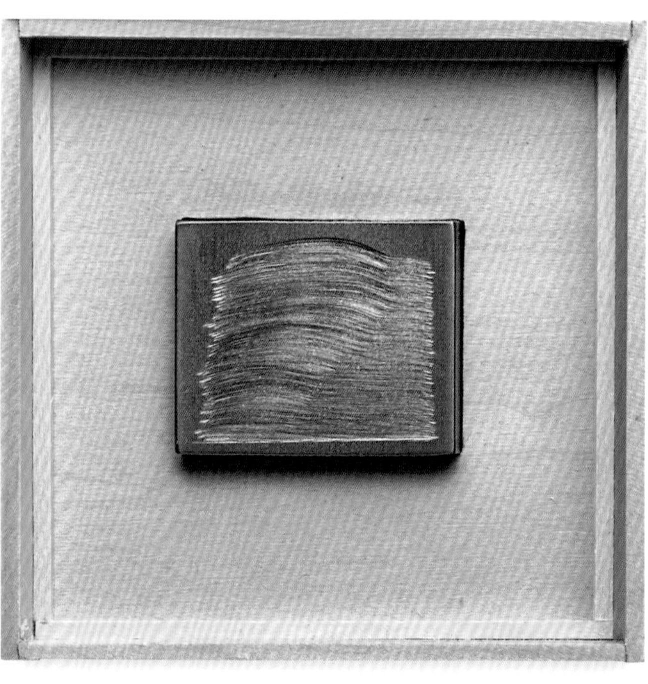

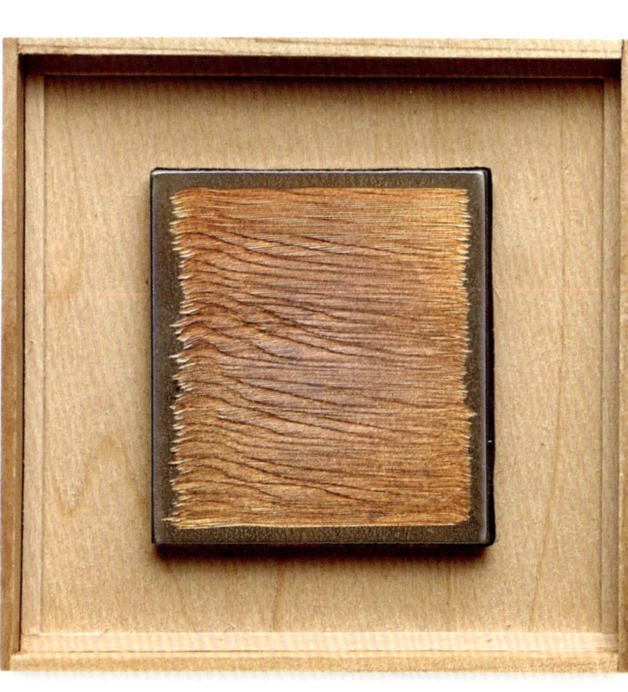

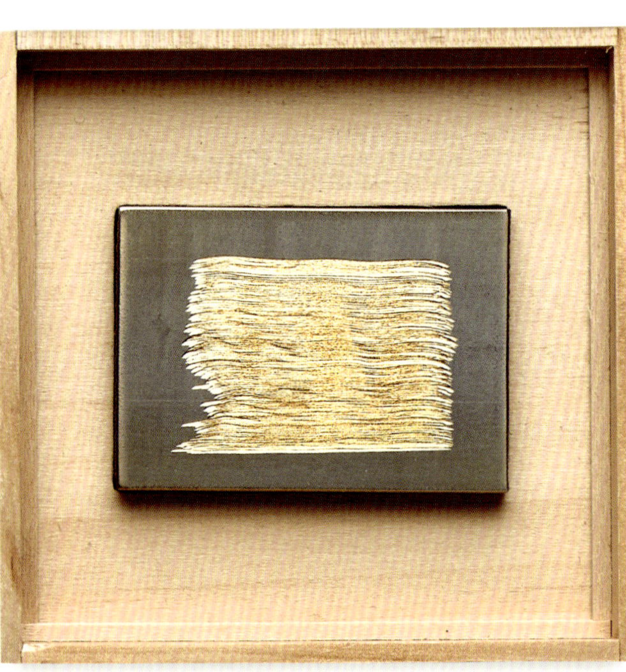

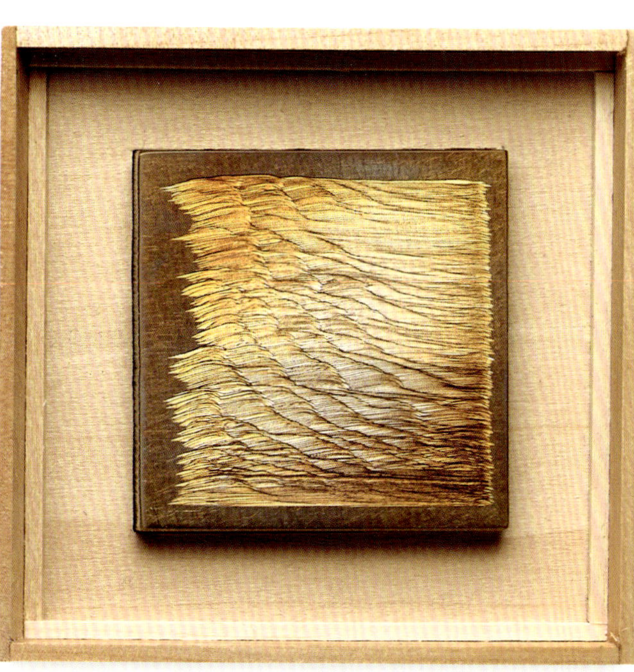

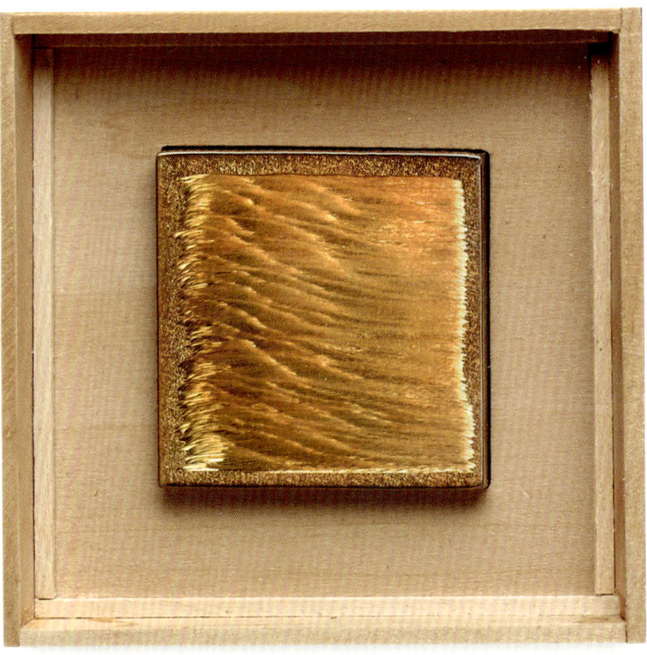

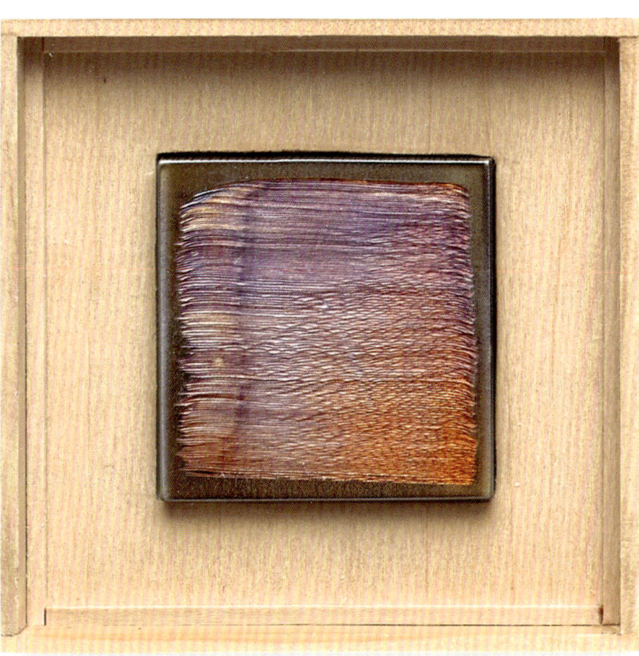

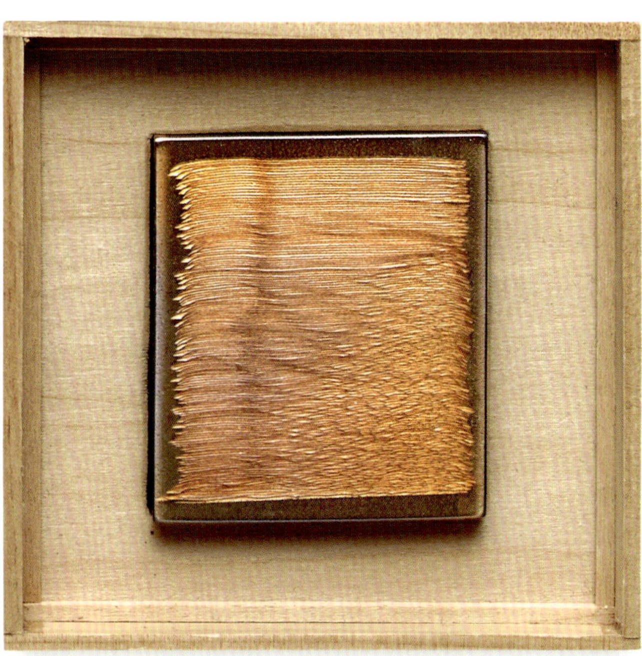

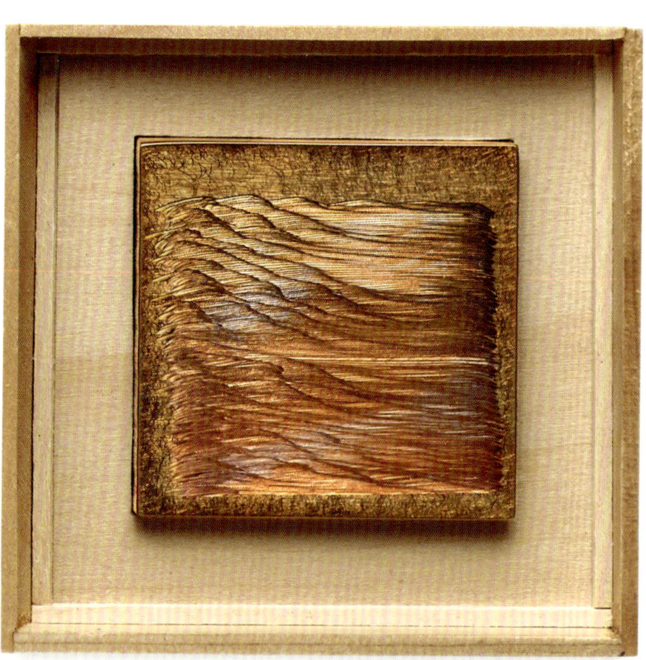

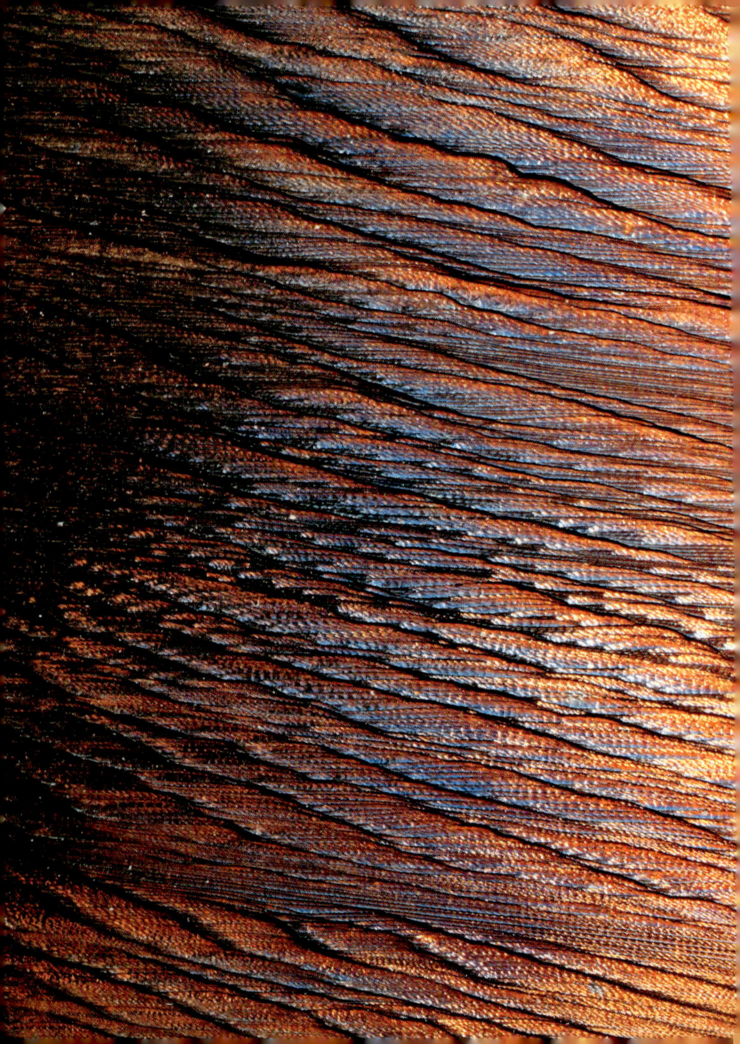

MATERIALS

bristol board
Davey archival binder's board
kiln-dried pine
modern full-cut diamonds
modern single-cut diamonds
old European diamonds
old mine-cut diamonds
paulownia
PVA glue
steel 216
steel 303
steel 316
steel 440C
steel 1018
steel 1215
steel 12L14
sugar pine
vegetable-tanned leather
wheat paste

Thinking about Monet
By Daniel Brush

Published on the occasion of the exhibition *Daniel Brush: Thinking about Monet*, presented by L'ÉCOLE, School of Jewelry Arts at 21_21 DESIGN SIGHT Gallery 3, Tokyo. January–April, 2024

Support for *Thinking about Monet* is provided by L'ÉCOLE, School of Jewelry Arts

First published by
L'ÉCOLE, School of Jewelry Arts
www.lecolevancleefarpels.com

and

MW Editions
www.mweditions.com
info@mweditions.com

Creative Direction and Design: Takaaki Matsumoto, Matsumoto Incorporated, New York
Design Assistant: Robin Brunelle, Matsumoto Incorporated, New York
Editor: Amy Wilkins, Matsumoto Incorporated, New York

Printed and bound by Conti Tipocolor, Italy
ISBN: 978-8-9877845-2-5

Library of Congress Control Number: 2023916502

Distribution
D.A.P. / Distributed Art Publishers, Inc.
75 Broad Street, Suite 630
New York, NY 10004
www.artbook.com
orders@dapinc.com